The Rabbit with Tl

Foreword

These stories were made up 'off-the-cuff' as bedtime tales for my grandson, Yannou.

Yannou often contributes to the stories from under the covers so it is new and exciting for both of us.

It is my greatest pleasure to see his little eyes widen with wonder as we hear of the rabbit's adventures.

I look forward to reading these stories to my new granddaughter, Elyssa, when she is a bit older.

GJ Abercrombie

Edinburgh

2018

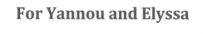

For Yannou and Elyssa

Chapter 1

Meet the Rabbit

The Rabbit with Three Ears lives in a flat on the 1st floor of a large building in Portobello, Scotland. He has three ears: one on the left side of his head, one on the right and one at the back. His ears are long and floppy and hang down beside (and behind) his body.

One night the Rabbit with Three Ears was in his flat and some mice were scuttling about under the floorboards. The mice were trying to steal the carrots which he had bought for his dinner. They were squeaking very quietly but the Rabbit with Three Ears heard them and chased them away.

"GET-OUT-OF-IT", he shouted and the mice all ran off.

The only reason he heard them was because having three ears made him very good at hearing.

Having three ears is very useful. Not only is your hearing very <u>good</u> but you can hear lots of different things at the same time. You can listen to the radio with one ear, listen to a programme on the TV with another ear and still have one spare to listen out for other things.

One night the Rabbit with Three Ears was doing just that. He was listening to some Beatles songs on the radio and watching an interesting programme about carrots on the TV.

Suddenly, he heard footsteps outside on the stairs up to his flat.

He heard this with his third ear.

It was a robber who was coming to trying to steal his stuff.

He opened his door and shouted "GET-OUT-OF-IT" and the robber ran away and never came back.

The rabbit went back inside and continued listening to his two programmes.

He liked having three ears!

Chapter 2

A Bad-Ear Day

Having three long floppy ears could also be a bit of a pest.

One windy day The Rabbit with Three Ears was walking along the road. The wind was blowing his three ears about all over the place. Suddenly, the wind blew his back ear right over the top of his head and down in front of his face. His eyes were covered and he could not see where he was going. He walked right into a lamppost and banged his head.

"GRRRRR" said the rabbit as he rubbed his sore head.

He tried using clothes pegs to stop them flying about but the pegs just kept pinging off with the wind.

Then he had a good idea about how to stop his ears flapping about. He put glue on them!

His ears were then very hard and stiff:

- The left one stuck straight out to his left
- the right one stuck straight out to his right
- the back one stuck straight up in the air from the back of his head

This certainly stopped them from flapping about and he was very pleased.

But, not for long …

When he tried to get into his car to drive to his work, he had a problem. His back ear (which was sticking right up in the air) banged into the roof of his car when he tried to get in the door.

He had to break the glue with a loud CRACK so that the ear did not stick up any more.

He managed to get into the car but when he tried to close the car door, his right ear kept hitting the window. Instead of breaking the glue on his right ear, he had another 'good idea'.

He rolled down the car window and drove to his work with his ear sticking out of the side of the car.

But, when he got to his work, he still had two ears sticking out at the side of his head and he could not fit in through the front door. He had to turn sideways to get into the building. He had to do this all day with every door at his work.

That night, he sat in the bath and used some nice warm water and soapy bubbles to wash the glue out of his ears.

Maybe the glue was not such a 'good idea' after all.

Chapter 3

Ear Mix-up

Did I mention that the Rabbit with Three Ears could take his ears off and put them on again?

No? Well, he can!

This makes it easier to wash them. He does not have to get into the bath to keep his three ears clean.

Did you know that the Rabbit with Three Ears has a name?

No? Well, it's TREVOR ……. Trevor, the Rabbit with Three Ears!

One day, Trevor (the Rabbit with Three Ears) had taken his ears off to wash them and then, by mistake, he put his left ear back on the right side of this head and his right ear on the left side. He did not notice this!

Then his friend, Declan, came into his flat and stood on Trevor's right-hand-side.

He shouted "Hey, Trevor!"

Trevor heard him in his left ear (which was on the right side, nearest to Declan) so he turned his head to the left to look for his friend. But Declan was not there!

Declan ran round to Trevor's left-hand-side and shouted "Hey, Trevor!" again. This time Trevor looked to the right because that's which ear he heard Declan's voice in.

This went on for a long time until Declan realised what was going on and grabbed Trevor by the shoulders.

"Your ears are mixed up!" said Declan.

"Oh, sorry Declan", said Trevor, "I took my ears off to wash them and must have put them back on the wrong way round. Silly me!"

Between them, they managed to sort out Trevor's ears and the Rabbit with Three Ears could hear properly again.

The two friends had a cup of tea and played a game of Dominos.

Chapter 4

Ear Thief

The next day, Trevor, the Rabbit with Three Ears, was going swimming. He decided to take his ears off so they would not get wet in the water. He left them in the changing room at the swimming pool.

Because he had no ears on, he could not hear anything. He did not hear when a sly fox went into the changing room and stole one of his ears.

The fox had always wanted to have three ears. He wanted to be like Trevor.

When Trevor came out of the pool after his swim, he noticed that one of his ears was missing. He looked around to see who might have taken it and saw someone sneaking out of the door but he could not see who it was.

Trevor went out into the pool's shop where they sell swimming trunks and goggles. Inside the shop, the fox was pretending to be just a normal fox (he had a hat over the third ear). There were lots of other animals in the shop so Trevor did not know which one had stolen his ear.

Then he had a 'good idea'.

He shouted, "Hey, Trevor!" and the fox heard him through Trevor's ear and, without thinking, said "Yes? What is it?"

"AHA!" shouted Trevor, "Got you, you thieving fox. Give me back my ear".

"But, I like having three ears" said the fox.

"Yes, so do I" said Trevor, "It's very useful sometimes. But these are MY ears and I need all three of them".

The fox gave Trevor his ear back and said he was sorry for stealing it.

I'm not sure the fox really was sorry because he still played tricks on Trevor, as we shall hear later!

Chapter 5

Seagull Trouble

Trevor, the Rabbit with Three Ears, was going out for a walk and he wanted to listen to some music.

He put on his headphones but they only had two earpieces. Now, Trevor has three ears so he could still hear the noise of all the lorries and buses and cars which were going past. He heard this through his third ear. The traffic noise was very annoying as it was spoiling his music.

Then he had a 'good idea'.

Trevor noticed that the two earpieces he had were round and soft and spongy so he decided he could make an extra earpiece for his third ear. He looked in the cupboard at home and found a bagel. It looked just ideal for an earpiece as it was also round and soft and spongy. He attached it to his headphones with some sticky tape and tried them on. It felt OK but when he went outside he could still hear the traffic. He realised that this was because the bagel had a hole in the middle of it. This hole was letting all the noise in.

He went back home and had another look in his cupboard. He found a Hot-Cross-Bun (which does not have a hole in the middle) and he stuck it in place instead of the bagel. Now, Trevor's Granny always called Hot-Cross-Buns 'HCBs', so Trevor called them that too.

The HCB was much better at blocking the noise and he could hear his music at last. He set off along the road but soon he started to hear cars and lorries and buses again.

"That's funny", he thought as the noise started to get louder. After a while he looked in the glass of a baker's shop window (which was like a mirror) and saw what was going on!

A big seagull was standing on Trevor's head pecking away at the HCB which was covering his third ear. The HCB had a big hole in it now, just like the bagel had!

Trevor thought very quickly and asked the seagull if he liked carrot-cake (Yannou's idea). "YUK", said the seagull, "No I don't like carrot-cake".

So Trevor went into the baker's shop and bought a slice of carrot-cake. He removed what was left of the HCB and gave it to the hungry seagull, who gobbled it all up. Trevor then replaced the HCB with the slice of carrot-cake he had just bought.

"Ah, that's much better", he said to himself.

Trevor listened to his music all the time he was out for a walk without any more trouble from pesky seagulls.

But, he had to wash his ears when he got home because one of them was all sticky from the icing on the carrot-cake.

Chapter 6

Declan-copter

Did I mention that Trevor's friend, Declan, has ten ears? *(TEN EARS!!)*

No? Well, he does!

They are evenly spaced around the top of his head and they all hang down like long hair. Sometimes Declan has to push the ears at the front apart so he can see out. Other times, he ties all his ears together in a bunch with a dark blue ribbon.

One day, Trevor (the Rabbit with Three Ears) and Declan (the Rabbit with Ten Ears) were at a party. All their friends were there and they were having great fun playing games. At one point, Trevor started spinning around very quickly and his three ears rose up and stuck out to the sides.

"Wee-Hee", he said, "This is great fun!"

"I'm going to try that", said Declan.

He removed the blue ribbon and started to spin around very fast. His ears all stuck out to the side, just like Trevor's ears had done.

But then something strange happened!

His ten spinning ears made him look like a helicopter as he spun faster and faster. Suddenly Declan started to lift off from the ground and rise into the air.

All their friends started to shriek with excitement at the sight of Declan flying.

Just before Declan's head hit the ceiling, Trevor grabbed his ankles and pulled him back down.

"You took off like a helicopter and nearly hit the ceiling" said Trevor, excitedly.

When Declan stopped spinning round he was a bit dizzy but after a while he recovered and managed to thank his friend, Trevor, for saving him from banging his head on the ceiling.

To this day, Declan is always very careful not to turn around too quickly in case he accidentally takes off like a helicopter again.

Chapter 7

Smelly Sock Swap

On a cold, wintry day, Trevor, the Rabbit with Three Ears was going out to the shops to buy something for his dinner.

It was so cold outside that he decided to wear his woolly hat. It was a fox hat *(the same as his friend Yannou has)* and it had two woolly flaps at the sides. These flaps were there to make sure the person wearing the hat had nice, cosy ears.

But Trevor had three ears and the hat only had two flaps!

Trevor had a 'good idea' *(again)*.

He took one of his socks from the wash basket and sewed it onto the hat to make a third flap.

He went off to the shops singing "La, La, La" to himself. As he passed some people on the way, they all started holding their noses and saying "Pooeee, what a smell!" Trevor realised that the sock he had sewn onto his hat had been worn on his smelly foot (the left one). It smelled of rotten fish and stinky cheese.

He rushed home and quickly found the other sock in the wash basket. It had been worn on his lovely foot (the right one) and smelled of flowers and custard.

Trevor quickly replaced the horrible, stinky sock with the lovely, perfumed sock and went back outside.

On his way back to the shops, everyone he met commented on how nice he smelled.

Some bees even followed him thinking he had some real flowers on his hat!

Trevor thought that having a lovely-smelling right foot made up for having a horrible, stinky left foot.

He was very happy (as well as very cosy) and he bought some tasty fish-fingers and a huge baked potato for his dinner.

Chapter 8

Declan Saves the Day

One sunny day in summer, Trevor and Declan decided to go on a boat trip on the loch. They borrowed a little boat with oars and an engine from a friend who lived beside the loch. She was happy to lend them her boat.

The rabbits started out rowing the boat with oars but they found that this was very hard work and the boat only moved across the water very slowly.

Then Trevor had a 'good idea'!

"Let's use the boat's engine, then we can go faster", he said. Soon the propeller was spinning round and they were zooming about on the loch. "Wee-Hee!" cried Trevor and Declan, "this is great fun!"

Suddenly, there was a loud bang and then "phut, phut, phut". The engine broke down and the propeller stopped turning. *(Yannou thinks the propeller must have become tangled in some weeds).* They were stuck out in the middle of the loch and it was too far to row to the shore.

"Oh No! What will we do?" cried Trevor.

Then Declan had a good idea (it was usually Trevor who had the good ideas, but this time it was Declan).

He said, "Remember when I spun around and my ten ears made me into a helicopter? Well, I wonder if I could make them into a propeller". He stuck his head into the water at the back of the boat and started to spin around while Trevor held onto his legs so he did not fall into the loch.

It worked a treat! The boat was soon zooming back to the shore.

As they got closer to the edge Trevor told Declan to spin a bit slower so that they did not crash into the wooden pier.

When they returned the boat to their friend they said they were sorry that the engine was broken.

"Don't worry," she said, "That has happened before and I think I know how to fix it."

Trevor and Declan thanked her for the loan of her boat and headed home.

When the two rabbit friends got back to Trevor's flat, Declan was still a bit dizzy from all the spinning.

Trevor made him a glass of orange squash and said, "Thanks Declan, you really saved the day".

Chapter 9

Pesky Pigeons

One wintry day, Trevor (the Rabbit with Three Ears) went to visit his friend Declan (the Rabbit with Ten Ears).

As he walked along the street, it began to snow and Trevor realised he had forgotten to bring his woolly fox hat.

(Do you remember this hat from a previous story?)

His head was getting very cold with the snow so he decided to make a hat out of his three ears. He pulled them all up over his head to form a nice, flat cover, like a tray, on his head. The snow was falling very quickly and soon there was a big pile of it on his head. The pile got bigger and bigger as more snow fell.

Soon Trevor started to notice that people were pointing at him and laughing but he could not work out why. Then he saw his reflection in a shop window. Some pigeons were using the snow on his head to make a snowman!

They were patting it into shape with their wings. One pigeon flew off to a vegetable shop and came back with a carrot for its nose; another found some big black buttons for its eyes; a third pigeon even found two old toothbrushes and stuck them in the sides of the body to make arms.

Trevor was annoyed!

The pigeons were making him look silly, so he shouted, "GET-OUT-OF-IT!" and shooed them away.

When he arrived at Declan's house, he could not fit in the door because the snowman on his head made him too tall. Declan had to push the snow off Trevor's head with a sweeping brush!

Trevor's ears were very cold and wet with the snow so Declan used a hair-dryer to dry them. The hot air also helped to warm up his ears and his head. Then Declan made his friend a nice cup of tea so his tummy was warm and cosy too.

As they drank their tea together Trevor and Declan worked out a plan to teach those naughty pigeons a lesson.

Declan suggested putting honey on their feet to stick them to the trees.

Trevor thought that putting maple syrup on their wings to stop them flying would be a good idea.

What do you think they should do?

We'll have to wait until the next story to find out what they did!

Chapter 10

The Rabbits' Revenge

As Trevor was finishing his cup of tea, he looked out of Declan's window and could see the pigeons strutting about pecking up seeds and nuts from the ground then flying up into the trees in the garden. They landed on the branches and sat fatly making their usual pigeon noises. This cooing drove the rabbits crazy (because, remember, they had thirteen ears between them); it sounded REALLY LOUD.

Suddenly, Trevor had a 'good idea' about how to trick them! He asked Declan if he had a tin of beans.

"Of course" said Declan, "all rabbits love eating beans. That's why we do so many pumpies! This helps us to run fast and jump over things."

"Great" said Trevor "here's what we'll do ..."

Trevor and Declan took some of the beans and washed the tomato sauce off of them. They then squashed each bean a little bit until they all had square corners. Finally they got some paint from Declan's art set and painted them yellow. Each bean now looked exactly like a bit of sweetcorn!

Now, pigeons LOVE eating sweetcorn!

When the pigeons weren't looking, the rabbits put some of their trick sweetcorn in the garden. Then they ran back into the house and hid behind the curtains to see what would happen.

The pigeons swooped down shouting "Look guys, yummy sweetcorn for us!" They gobbled them all up quickly.

Soon the beans started to take effect!

One pigeon did a big pumpy as he flew up into the trees and missed his branch. He landed in a big muddy puddle!

Another one took off and flew up to a tree but just as he was about to land, he did a pumpy too. He crashed into the tree trunk and bashed his beak.

As a third pigeon was about to take off, he did a huge pumpy and shot off into the sky like a rocket and landed on the roof of Declan's house!

Pigeons are not used to eating beans.

Trevor and Declan saw all of this from inside the house and laughed and laughed!

"That serves them right for making a snowman on my head; those cheeky pigeons", said Declan.

"Listen!" said Trevor.

"What?" said Declan, "I can't hear anything."

"Exactly! No more cooing … Ahh, that's lovely and quiet. Let's have another cup of tea!"

Chapter 11

Flying Declan

Do you remember the party where Declan spun round and took off like a helicopter?

Well, one day he decided he'd like to try it again, but this time he would do it outside so he did not bang his head on the ceiling inside the house. He thought it would be best to get help from his friend Trevor (the Rabbit with Three Ears) in case he flew too high. He went round to Trevor's house to ask him if he was busy.

Trevor was delighted to help. He suggested that they should tie a bit of string to Declan's foot so that Trevor could hold onto it to stop him flying away. Declan spun around as fast as he could and soon he was up, up, up in the air.

"Wee-Hee!" he yelled as Trevor held on tightly to the string.

"I can see my house from up here", Declan shouted as he flew above the trees in Trevor's back garden. He could even see the fat, pumpy pigeons that they had tricked before!

Now, Trevor wanted to try flying too so he pulled the string to bring Declan back down. Declan slowed his spinning down and landed with a slight bump on the grass beside Trevor.

"That was GREAT!" Declan cried.

"Let me try," said Trevor.

So they tied the bit of string to Trevor's foot (the nice-smelling, right one, not the stinky, left one) and he started to spin around. He spun and he spun as fast as he could but he could not get off the ground.

He tried running very fast and jumping up into the air. No luck!

He tried jumping off of a kitchen chair. Still no luck!

He simply could not fly!

"It's because I've only got three ears", he cried. "<u>You</u> can fly because you've got ten ears", he told Declan.

Trevor was not happy for a while … but then he had one of his 'good ideas'!

I wonder what it was … do you?

We'll find out next time!

Chapter 12

Trevor Takes to the Air

Since Trevor's three ears did not have enough power to lift him off of the ground, he decided to buy a REAL helicopter!

He went to the shop and chose a nice shiny red one with the number 3 on the front and the sides.

(I wonder why he chose the number 3.)

He took a few flying lessons and then decided to show Declan his new helicopter. He flew over the trees and landed in his friend's garden. As he landed, the strong wind from the helicopter's blades blew the fat pigeons (FPs) right off the branches of the 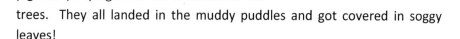 trees. They all landed in the muddy puddles and got covered in soggy leaves!

Declan heard the noise of the helicopter and the loud, angry cooing of the FPs (fat pigeons) and he came running out of the house to see what was going on. When he saw Trevor's helicopter, he was excited.

"Yippee", said Declan, "Now we can go flying together!"

Declan had been practising his spin-flying and so he did not need the string around his foot anymore. The two friends flew off into the air, heading for the Pirate Park in Portobello. When they got there, they landed just outside the gate because *(as you know)* you are not allowed to land helicopters inside the playpark. They had great fun on the slide, the see-saw and the spinny-round thing with seats on it. *(what's it called?)*

Trevor was pleased to spin round on it because all the dirt from his three ears flew off and landed in the flowerbeds. His ears were very dirty because he had spent so much time learning how to fly his new helicopter that he had not had time to wash them!

He had so much dirt in his ears that his Granny said she could grow potatoes in them!

Eventually it was time to go home and Trevor ran to his lovely red flying machine. He jumped into the pilot's seat and was just about to start the engine when he heard Declan crying. *(You don't have to have three ears to know when your friend is sad).*

"What's wrong?" he asked his chum and Declan looked at him with tears in his eyes.

"It's my neck", he sobbed, "It's so sore with all the spinning around I did. I don't think I'll be able to fly home".

"Don't be sad," said Trevor, "There's a spare seat beside me in the helicopter".

Declan smiled, dried his tears with two of his ears and jumped up into the passenger seat. Then the two friends flew home together listening to songs by the Beatles on the CD player and singing along loudly to try to drown out the noise of the helicopter's blades.

Having so many ears, they found the noise inside the helicopter very loud.

They decided that one day they would think of a 'good idea' to try to block out the noise.

What do YOU think they could do?

Chapter 13

Shoe Search

When Trevor got home to his house, he discovered he had forgotten something ... his shoes!

He had taken them off at the Pirate Park so he could zoom down the slide without his shoes sticking.

His socks were much slippier and faster.

Anyway, he flew back to the park to get his shoes but when he got there, they were gone! Someone had stolen them *(I wonder who?)* He asked all the other animals who were in the park if anyone knew who had taken his shoes; but no-one had seen anything.

Then a big dog came over and said he had a very sensitive nose and he could follow things by their smell. Luckily, Trevor has very smelly feet (one nice, one horrible) so his shoes would leave a very strong trail for the dog to follow. The dog sniffed the ground, starting from the bottom of the slide, where Trevor had left his shoes.

"Oh Yes!" he said "I can definitely smell something nice and something stinky".

The dog started running off following the scent of the missing shoes with Trevor running behind him (in his socks).

Eventually, the dog came to a halt outside the door of a house. They rang the doorbell and *who do you think opened the door? ...*

It was the fox who had stolen Trevor's ear at the swimming pool!

Trevor said, "Eh, hello. Have you stolen my shoes?"

"No" said the fox, but when Trevor looked down, there on the fox's feet were Trevor's shoes!

"Give me back my shoes", said Trevor and the big dog started to growl.

The fox said "Sorry" (again, just like he did about the stolen ear before).

(Yannou says that the fox could go to the Gyle and buy some shoes for himself as there are lots of shoe-shops there.)

Anyway, Trevor got his shoes back. He thanked the big dog (whose name he did not know) and flew back home in his helicopter.

It's a good thing his feet are so smelly or else he may not have got his shoes back.

Chapter 14

Beach Picnic

One sunny day, Trevor and Declan (the rabbits with many, many ears between them) decided to go to the beach!

They packed a picnic of cold sausages, crisps, apples and ham sandwiches in a little rucksack. They also packed some orange squash to drink and a big sheet from Trevor's bed to sit on. Trevor put the rucksack on his back and they ran outside to get into the helicopter to fly to the beach. Trevor jumped up into the pilot's seat and his friend Declan took the passenger seat beside him.

"Off we GO!" shouted Trevor excitedly.

But when he turned the key to start the helicopter's engine, nothing happened! The battery was flat.

"Oh dear, how will we get to the beach now?" said Declan.

They got out of the helicopter and lay down on the grass, both feeling very sad. Trevor looked up and saw lots of little white clouds scudding across the sky. He noticed that they were heading in the direction of the beach and suddenly he had one of his 'good ideas'.

He pulled the sheet out of his rucksack and shouted to Declan to hold two of the corners. Trevor grabbed the other two corners and they threw the sheet up into the air like a fishing-net.

After a few tries, they managed to catch a little cloud in the sheet and were pulled along with the wind.

"Hang on tight" shouted Trevor, and soon the two rabbits were flying over the fences and hedges towards the beach!

"Woo-Hoo!" they cried.

When they got to the beach, Trevor let go of his end of the sheet and landed on the sand but Declan was too slow. The cloud carried him right over the sand and he landed in the sea. Declan was still holding onto the sheet which was now soaking wet.

And so was poor Declan.

Don't worry; the water was not very deep, only up to his waist. He walked out of the sea and up the beach to where Trevor was waiting. Trevor was laughing so hard that his ears were flapping about like three flags on one flagpole.

"GRRRRR!" said Declan, but then he started to laugh too.

They held the sheet up high in the air with their ears (luckily they had thirteen ears between them) and the wind blew it dry in a few minutes.

The two friends had a lovely day at the beach, eating their picnic on the nice clean sheet which had been washed in the sea and dried in the wind.

But … how were they going to get home from the beach? They could not catch a cloud again as the wind was still blowing out to sea.

Find out next time!

Chapter 15

Tunnel Travel

Trevor and Declan had finished their picnic and were sitting on the clean sheet on the beach wondering how they were going to get home.

Then suddenly they noticed the sand in front of them starting to move. It rose into a little hill and out popped a brown face. It was their friend the mole. His name was Dig-Down Dirty because he dug down into the ground and so was very dirty. *(Yannou's idea)*

He liked his friends to call him Dig-Down 'D' as he did not want to be thought of as 'dirty'.

He said to Trevor and Declan, "I'm about to dig a tunnel back to my house and I will be passing Declan's house in Leith on the way. Do you want to follow me underground?"

"That would be great", said the rabbits, "but we've never been in a mole's tunnel before."

"That's OK" said Dig-Down 'D', "Just follow me closely and hold the tunnel roof up with your ears. You can let the dirt fall down behind you as we travel along."

So off they set from the beach; Dig-Down 'D' pushing the ground aside to make a tunnel, Trevor with his rucksack on his back holding the tunnel roof up with his three ears and Declan at the back using five of his ears to hold up the roof and the other five to fill in the tunnel behind them.

Very soon, they arrived at Declan's house. They came up through a little hole in the floor of his basement. Trevor and Declan thanked their friend for his help and Dig-Down 'D' set off again, digging a little tunnel back to his own house.

On the way, he sang his favourite tunnelling song:

Dig-Down Dirty that's me

I tunnel as fast as can be

I zoom underground

Hardly making a sound

And my friends call me Dig-Down 'D'

Back in Leith, Declan reminded Trevor to buy a new battery for his helicopter and the two rabbits said "goodbye".

Trevor ran home and made a cup of tea before getting into his bed.

It was a bit scratchy because there was still a lot of sand stuck to his clean sheet!

Chapter 16

A Shocking Pigeon Story

The next morning, Trevor remembered that he needed to buy a new battery for his helicopter so he walked along to the shops.

Now, helicopter batteries are not like the little ones you put in a toy lightsabre; they are big and heavy. Trevor could not carry it all the way home and it was too big to fit into his rucksack. The shopkeeper said he would normally have offered to help carry it home but he was too busy painting a shelf in the shop.

Trevor asked the shopkeeper if he could borrow a shopping trolley to take the battery home. The shopkeeper said "Of course, Trevor. As long as you bring the trolley back" and then he got on with his painting.

Trevor said "Thanks" and promised to bring back the trolley.

He was walking home with the new battery in the trolley when a fat pigeon (FP) flew down and landed in front of him. The pigeon had meant to land in the trolley but it landed on the battery instead and got an electric shock!

"DDDZZZZZZZZZZZZZZTT!"

The pigeon's feathers stuck out all over the place and its wings flew up over its head. It looked more like a hedgehog than a pigeon. There was also some smoke coming from its tail and Trevor could smell burning.

The pigeon was starting to catch fire!

Trevor ran back into the shop and used his three ears to scoop up some water out of a fish tank. He ran to the door with the water in his ear-cup but he tripped on the step and fell over. The water splashed onto the pavement.

Trevor ran back into the shop shouting:

"Help! Has anyone got any liquid that I can use to put out a burning pigeon?"

The shopkeeper gave him the first thing that came to hand. It was the tin of yellow paint which he had been using to paint his shelf.

Trevor ran back outside and chucked the paint all over the pigeon. This put the fire out with a loud HISSSSSSSS!

The pigeon was no longer on fire but it was covered in yellow paint.

Trevor took the pigeon home with him, put the new battery in his helicopter and flew to the hospital with the pigeon. The doctors at the hospital used special cream to get all of the yellow paint out of the pigeon's feathers but they could not get it to come off of his beak.

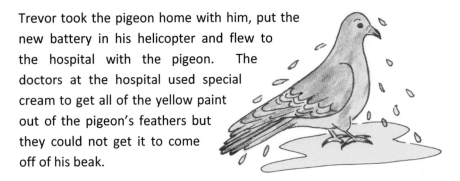

So if you ever see a pigeon with a yellow beak, it might be the one who landed on Trevor's battery.

Chapter 17

The Noisy Neighbour

As you know, Trevor, the Rabbit with Three Ears lives in a flat on the 1st floor of a large building in Portobello, Scotland.

It was time for Trevor to wash his ears so he took them off and put them in his bathtub full of soapy water. He was busy scrubbing away when he started to sing his favourite song.

"La, La, La," he sang to himself.

When his ears were clean, he put them back on, one at a time. After his first ear was on, he heard a quiet knocking noise (knock, knock, knock); when he put on his second ear, the knocking got louder (KNOCK, KNOCK, KNOCK). When all three of his ears were on and he could hear properly he realised that the knocking noise was someone banging at his front door! When he opened the door, there stood one of his neighbours, Mrs O'Hare; she was very angry indeed.

"Trevor," she said "Have you been singing with your ears off again?"

Then Trevor remembered that without his ears he could not hear anything and so he did not realise how LOUDLY he was singing. All the rabbits in the other flats had been holding their ears because of the racket he was making.

And, even worse, it meant that they could not hear their own TV programmes!

Trevor said that he was sorry to Mrs O'Hare and that he would try to remember in future only to sing with at least two of his three ears on.

After a few minutes, he heard another knock as his door. When he opened it up, he saw ANOTHER one of his neighbours (not Mrs O'Hare) standing there. The neighbour said that she had heard the singing and, although it was a bit loud, it was actually very nice to listen to.

When he closed the door, he started singing his favourite "La, La, La" song again, but this time he could hear himself and so did not sing too loudly and did not disturb anyone.

Trevor was very pleased that one of his neighbours thought that he was a good singer!

Chapter 18

The Dancing Rabbit Chorus

The next morning, when Trevor was having his breakfast, he could hear his neighbours in the other flats. Some of them were eating noisy cereals which went 'SNAP – CRACKLE – POP'. Others were humming to themselves or singing along with the radio.

Trevor could hear them all; not because they were singing loudly, but because he has three ears. Having three ears makes you able to hear really well. And remember, he had just washed his ears the night before so they were very clean and working really well!

He noticed that the neighbours were each singing different songs and so it all sounded a bit jumbled up to Trevor.

Then he had one of his 'good ideas'.

After breakfast, he asked all of his neighbours to meet in the garden at the back of the flats and then he got each rabbit to teach everyone else their favourite song:

- Someone liked 'Jingle Bells'
- Someone else liked the Darth Vader theme from Star Wars
- Another liked 'Octopus's Garden' by the Beatles

Very soon, all of the neighbours were singing along together and Trevor was very impressed!

"You sound great!" he said.

"Maybe we should form a choir," said Mrs O'Hare, "we could call it The Portobello Rabbit Chorus".

Just then, Trevor's friend Declan appeared. Declan, is also a rabbit but he has ten ears! He lives in a little house with a garden in Leith which is not too far from Portobello.

Because he has ten ears, Declan could hear the singing all the way from Leith.

"What beautiful singing," he said, "can I join in too?"

"Of course you can" they all replied and taught Declan a few of their favourite songs.

Declan loved it so much that he asked if they could change the name of the choir to "The Portobello and Leith Rabbit Chorus", because he lives in Leith.

The other rabbits said that this would be OK.

When Declan started to sing, everyone got a big surprise. His voice was very, very deep. It was so low and booming that the ground started to shake. The vibrating ground tickled the rabbits' feet and they all started to dance around as they sang.

Trevor shouted, "We're not just a chorus, we're a dance group too!"

Mrs O'Hare said, "Maybe we should be called the 'Portobello and Leith Dancing Rabbit Chorus'"

Everyone thought that the name was getting a bit too long so they agreed to shorten it to:

"The Dancing Rabbit Chorus"

Chapter 19

Rabbits in Disguise

"Oh dear, h...
three ear...
Then...
so...

Do you remember the fox who stole Trevor's

Well he decided to play a trick on Trevor. He put on a false mus...
and a policeman's hat to pretend
he was a policeman.

He went along to Declan's house
in Leith one night when the
Dancing Rabbit Chorus were
there, practising their singing
and dancing. He knocked on the
door and when Declan answered,
he said:

"Hello, I'm a policeman and I've come here to arrest a rabbit called Trevor
and take him to jail!"

Declan was shocked and worried for his friend. He could not imagine
what Trevor could have done wrong. He did not know why the police
would want to arrest him.

But Declan knew he had to try to help his friend to escape.

He said to the foxy-policeman, "Oh really, and what does this 'Trevor' look
like?"

"Well, he's a rabbit and he has three ears", replied the policeman/fox.

"OK, I'll see if I can find him", said Declan, "You wait here a minute" and
he left the police-fox at the door and ran inside.

He quickly explained what was happening to all the other rabbits. They
were all very worried for Trevor and then Mrs O'Hare said:

...ll know which one is Trevor because he's the only rabbit with ...!"

Trevor had a 'good idea' (again). He asked Declan if he could borrow ...ne of his ears (remember, Declan has ten ears).

Declan took off seven of his ears which left him with three. Trevor passed the spare ears to some of the other rabbits. Each rabbit stuck one of Declan's ears on beside their own two to give them three ears as well!

When they were ready, Declan shouted out to the 'pretend policeman' who was waiting at the door, "OK, you can come in now, Mr Policeman!"

The fox entered the living-room and saw nine rabbits with three ears! Declan, Trevor and seven other rabbits all had three ears each.

The fox was very confused and said, "Which one of you is Trevor, the Rabbit with Three Ears?"

Each of the friends took it in turn to say:

"I'm Trevor"

"I'm Trevor"

"I'm Trevor"

The fox was even more confused and ran around checking all the rabbits. He could not understand what was going on!

He eventually got so dizzy and tired with running and chasing the rabbits that he decided he needed a rest. He saw a big chair in Declan's living-room and ran over to sit on it. But just before he got to it, Trevor (the REAL Trevor) stuck a whoopee-cushion on it. When the fox sat on it, it made a huge pumpy sound:

PPPPPPFFFFFFFFFFFFTTTTTTTTT!

The fox got such a fright that the false moustache and hat fell off and everyone could see that he was not a real policeman, just a fox dressed up!

Mrs O'Hare said she was very pleased that Trevor was not really going to be arrested and go to jail.

The rabbits gave Declan back the ears they had borrowed and the fox had to say 'sorry' to Trevor (again!)

They can be terribly naughty, those foxes.

Just to show that they were not really too angry with the fox, the rabbits gave him a concert. They sang him a few of their favourite songs and did some of their best dances.

Chapter 20

Chorus Leader

After the tricky fox had gone away, The Dancing Rabbit Chorus started to practise their singing again.

Mrs O'Hare said they should choose a chorus leader.

"Some choirs call them Directors or Conductors, but I think we should keep it simple and call him (OR HER) the 'Chorus Leader'", she said. She seemed to say 'OR HER' quite loudly. *I wonder why?*

One of the other rabbits asked her what the leader would have to do; what is his (OR HER) job?

"Well", said Mrs O'Hare, "he (OR SHE) would make sure the chorus were all singing together by checking:

- That they were all singing the same song for a start. That's very important!
- That they were all singing at the same speed. You don't want some rabbits getting to the end of the song before the others.
- That any rabbits whose ears can come off have got them all on. She looked straight at Trevor when she said this!

Trevor said, "Hey, what about Declan? His ears come off too!"

"Yes, but Declan remembers not to sing LOUDLY while his ears are off!" she replied. Some of the other rabbits giggled when she said this!

One of the young rabbits suggested that Trevor should be the leader as it was he who got the chorus together in the first place.

"But, I don't know how to conduct a chorus!" said Trevor.

"You just stand out in front of everyone and wave your arms about", said Mrs O'Hare. "It's easy. I used to do it at the school when I was a teacher".

(Did you know that Mrs O'Hare used to be a school teacher? No, neither did I!)

So, Trevor went to the front of the chorus and turned around to face them but when he waved his arms about, they kept getting tangled up in his long ears. "Oh, this is useless", said Trevor through a jumble of arms and ears.

He said, "Why don't you try conducting, Declan?" (Remember Declan uses a dark blue ribbon to tie his ears up.)

But Declan said he didn't fancy the idea of being the chorus leader, he preferred to be a singer.

Declan said, "Why doesn't Mrs O'Hare do it since she's done it before?"

All the rabbits thought that this was a 'good idea' and I think that's what Mrs O'Hare had hoped for when she first suggested having a chorus leader. *Don't you?*

Mrs O'Hare went back to her own flat for a minute and returned with what looked to Trevor like a big, long stick.

"This is the baton I used when I conducted the school choir", she told them all.

Declan and some other rabbits sang the low notes of the songs while Trevor and the rest sang the high notes.

Mrs O'Hare waved her arms about like a rabbit-windmill at the front.

She had a huge smile on her face.

Everyone was happy as they danced and sang together.

Chapter 21

The Surprise Cake

Trevor decided to bake his favourite cake: Banana Cake. It was one his Granny always used to bake for him and he had asked her for a copy of her recipe.

He carefully measured out the flour and butter and mixed them in a bowl with some eggs and, of course, mashed up bananas. He also added some milk to make sure the mixture was nice and sloppy.

When Trevor turned round to check that the oven was on, he did not notice that the ear on the back of his head dipped into the bowl with the cake mixture in it. His ear was a gooey mess but he did not notice because it was behind him.

He finished baking his cake and decided he would take some round to his friend Declan's house.

Now, it was a hot, sunny day and when Trevor went outside, the sun started to bake the cake mixture on his ear, just like in an oven.

Soon Trevor started to smell a lovely baking smell, but he thought it was just the bit of cake he had brought for Declan.

Later, as he was walking through the park, he noticed a big line of ducks behind him. He wondered what was going on.

"Why are you ducks all following me?" he asked them.

"Because we would like some of your yummy cake" they said.

"Sorry, this cake is for Declan", said Trevor, holding up the cake he had in his hands.

"No! Not that one; this one!" said the ducks, pointing at Trevor's back.

"Which one?" said Trevor turning around. He could not see the cake at his back because every time he turned round, the cake stayed behind him, on his third ear.

Finally, one of the ducks could not wait any longer. The smell of the yummy cake was too much for him. He flew up and tried to bite a bit of the cake but he pecked Trevor's ear by mistake.

"OW! AYAH!" said Trevor but he then realised what the ducks were talking about. He pulled off his ear which by this time had a beautifully cooked bit of Banana Cake on the end of it.

Trevor found a nice clean twig and took a big leaf from a nearby tree. He used the twig to scrape the cake off of his ear onto the leaf which made a good plate.

The ducks all stood round the leaf/plate in a circle and were just about to gobble up all the cake when a little duckling amongst them said that it was her birthday!

Because Trevor is a good singer *(he's in The Dancing Rabbit Chorus, you know)* he started singing 'Happy Birthday to You' and all the other ducks joined in.

The little duckling was very happy because they were all singing for her birthday and then the ducks ate up every crumb of the cake.

Trevor washed his ear in the pond in the park and ran all the way to Declan's house with his cake present.

The weather was still hot and sunny so they did not have a cup of tea with the cake. They each had a glass of cold milk instead.

Chapter 22

More Ear Trouble

Do you remember what Declan uses to tie up his ten ears? That's right, a dark blue ribbon.

Well, he was having a lot of trouble; the ribbon kept snapping and letting his ears fall down all around his head. When his front ears fell down and covered his eyes, he could not see anything.

This happened one night at the end of his favourite TV programme, Scooby-Doo. He missed the unmasking of the baddie and had to rewind the programme and watch that bit again after he had tied his ears back up.

Another time, the ribbon snapped while he was walking down the stairs and he tripped and fell down. Luckily he was near the bottom so he was not hurt too much.

When he told his friend Trevor about this, Trevor said "You must do something about that ribbon, Declan. Stairs are very dangerous if you can't see properly."

Then Trevor had a 'good idea'.

He remembered he'd seen a man called Bob Marley on the TV. Bob had lots of very long twisty hair which looked just like Declan's ears. He used to stuff all his hair into a big woolly hat to keep it tidy. Bob Marley's hat had many colours: Red, Yellow, Green and Black to represent the colours on the flags of countries which were important to him.

Trevor asked his Granny if she could knit a big hat like that for Declan. He asked her to make it blue and white, the colours of the Scottish flag because Trevor and Declan both lived in Scotland. Trevor's Granny is a very fast knitter so the hat was ready in two days, just in time for Declan's birthday! *(That was lucky.)*

Trevor gave his friend the hat as a present and Declan tried it on straight away. He pushed all ten of his ears into the hat and had a look at himself in the mirror. He thought he looked great in his new hat!

Trevor said, "Would you like to go out to a café for lunch for your birthday treat?"

No reply!

Trevor tried again, a bit louder.

"Declan, would you like to go out to a café for lunch for your birthday treat?"

No reply, again!

Trevor tried one more time, even LOUDER.

"Declan, would you like to go out to a café for lunch for your birthday treat?"

Finally, Trevor realised what was happening: Declan could not hear a thing with the new hat over all of his ears. Trevor pulled the hat off of Declan's head and all of his ears flopped down again.

"You could not hear me shouting", said Trevor.

"No", said Declan, "the hat is very smart to look at but, to tell you the truth; it makes my head a bit too hot".

"And it makes you deaf too!"

"Pardon?" said Declan, pretending he still could not hear!

The two friends had a good laugh at that joke.

Then Declan had a 'good idea'.

"Since the hat made my head very warm, maybe we could use it as a tea-cosy!" he said. So they put the hat over Declan's teapot and it kept the tea nice and hot for ages.

Trevor thought of a way to fix the problem with Declan's ears: he should use two ribbons at the same time.

Declan chose one blue ribbon and one white one so that it would look like the Scottish flag to remind him of the nice hat Trevor had given him for his birthday.

Chapter 23

Locked Out

Trevor was having his breakfast in his flat in Portobello. He had a nice hot cup of tea and a hot hot-cross-bun *(or an H-HCB as his Granny would call it)*.

Before he sat down to have this delicious meal he went out to put some rubbish into the recycling boxes which were kept on the landing shared with all the other flats in his building. Unfortunately, Trevor had left the kitchen window open and the wind blew in and shut his front door behind him with a loud 'SLAM"!

"OH NO!" he shouted, "I don't have my key with me!"

He ran down into the back garden and looked up at the open kitchen window which was much too high for him to reach. A few of the rabbits from the other flats heard the door slam and came out to see what was going on.

His friend Declan arrived from Leith too.

"I've locked myself out", cried Trevor "and my yummy breakfast is on the table!"

Then Declan had a 'good idea'. He stood against the wall under the open window and got one of the other rabbits to stand on his shoulders. Then a second rabbit jumped up on top to make the pile higher.

"Pile on!" shouted Declan and soon there was a long ladder made up of rabbits stretching up towards Trevor's kitchen window.

"OK, Trevor, climb up the rabbit-mountain!" said Declan.

Trevor started to make his way up the squirming pile of rabbits. His feet stood on shoulders and heads and arms and faces as he went higher and higher. Then, unfortunately, his smelly foot (the left one) landed on the nose of a rabbit near the top.

That unlucky rabbit was nearly sick from the awful smell! He did a huge cough and a sneeze and a pumpy, all at the same time. The whole rabbit-ladder collapsed on top of poor Declan. Luckily his ten ears made a nice furry cushion for the rabbits to land on. The ear-cushion also protected Declan's head so no-one was hurt.

"That awful, smelly foot of yours," said Declan "you need to do something about it".

Trevor had another 'good idea'. He took the sock off of his lovely-smelling foot (the right one) and covered the smelly foot with it to try to hide the stink.

"Right, let's try again", he said and the rabbit-ladder was re-built. Trevor started to climb again.

Some of the rabbits still turned their noses away as he passed; just in case! Soon Trevor reached the top of rabbit-mountain and could reach his kitchen window.

He jumped inside and opened the front door to let Declan and all the other rabbits in. They had climbed up the stairs and were pretty tired from being ladders.

"Come in everybody," said Trevor, "I'll make us all a cup of tea. I'll need to make a new pot anyway since my breakfast is cold".

As the rabbits all sat around drinking hot tea, one little one said "It's lucky we made a ladder and not a snake or else Trevor would have slid all the way down; like in the game 'Snakes and Ladders'".

The rabbits were all laughing at this joke when Declan said:

"Hey, I forgot! I could have used my ears like a helicopter and flown up to the open window. Silly me!"

and then Trevor said,

"Oops, I've just remembered that Mrs O'Hare has a spare key for my flat. I could have just asked her for it and opened the door. Silly me too!"

But that would not have been as much fun as building a rabbit-ladder.

Chapter 24

Ear Wars

Trevor and Declan had gone to the cinema to see the new Lego Star Wars movie. They both liked building things with Lego and they also loved all the Star Wars stories, so this was the perfect film for them to see.

Just as the film was about to start, the rabbit sitting directly behind Declan tapped him on the shoulder.

"Excuse me", she said "but I can't see the screen because of your ears being tied up like that. Can you please take them down?"

"Oh, I'm sorry", said Declan and he untied the blue and white ribbons which held up his ten ears. They immediately flopped down all around his body and in front of his face. He could not see the film any more.

Then he had a 'good idea'. He tied his front two ears around the sides of his head with the ribbons. Everyone was happy; Declan and the other rabbit could both see the film.

But, not for long!

Something very strange started happening. As the film got more and more interesting, Trevor and Declan got more and more excited; so excited that their ears stuck straight up in the air. Trevor's three ears made it hard for the rabbit behind him to see much of the screen but the rabbit behind Declan could see nothing at all!

She was NOT pleased.

Even the two front ears which he had tied back with ribbons were sticking up like lampposts and the ribbons had pinged off and hit the other rabbit on the face!

"Go and sit somewhere else", she shouted.

Trevor and Declan moved along the row a bit but the rabbits sitting behind these new seats were not happy either (and they were not as polite as the first rabbit had been).

Then it was Trevor's turn to have a 'good idea'.

"If we sit in the back row of the cinema, there will be NO rabbits behind us!" he said.

"Very clever", said Declan.

On their way to the back of the cinema they saw a little shop selling carrot ice-cream (their favourite) so Trevor bought a tub for each of them.

They enjoyed the film very much and found that being in the back row meant that they were nearest the doors and got out of the cinema first when the film was finished. This also meant that they were first in the queue for the bus which took them back home.

The friends decided that they would always sit in the back row of the cinema in future.

Chapter 25

Scaffies

Trevor was riding his bike one sunny day. He got to the top of a big, steep hill and prepared himself for a great, speedy ride to the bottom.

"Wee-Hee", he shouted as he sped down the hill. His three ears were flapping behind him as he went.

Suddenly, his left ear became unstuck and flew off; he had not attached it properly after his bath that morning!

He managed to stop his bike at the bottom of the hill and he looked back the way he had come. He could just see his ear lying on the road near the top of the hill. He started to push his bike all the way back up the hill. When he was half-way up, he saw a woman come out of her house and pick up his missing ear. She didn't know what it was so she just stuck it in her dustbin!

"Hey, that's my ear!" he shouted, but she was too far away to hear him.

He pushed his bike faster and faster up the hill but, before he reached the bin, the scaffies arrived; *(Scaffies are what Trevor's Granny calls dustbin men because she comes from Aberdeen).*

The bin lorry stopped beside the bin which had Trevor's ear in it and then the scaffy emptied the whole lot into the back of the lorry!

"Hey, my ear's in there!" Trevor shouted again, but the scaffies did not hear him because of the noise the lorry was making. They drove off just as Trevor reached them.

He jumped on his bike and chased the lorry but it was too fast. Trevor could not catch up with it.

He managed to keep sight of it all the way to the tip where the bin-lorries empty all the rubbish out onto big piles. Trevor saw the lorry go into the tip but he did not know where it had dumped his ear.

He was walking about on top of huge piles of smelly, stinky rubbish, so now BOTH of his feet smelled awful!

There were lots of noisy seagulls flying about over the tip and Trevor recognised the one who had been eating his hot-cross-bun (HCB) when he tried to use it as an earpiece on his headphones. He asked the seagull to help him to find his missing ear and the seagull said:

"Yes, I remember you. You kindly gave me a delicious HCB to eat. I'll see if I can find your ear".

The seagull flew up high and soon he spotted Trevor's ear in the pile of rubbish. He picked it up with his beak and flew back to Trevor with it.

Trevor thanked the seagull and jumped back on his bike. He did not put his ear back on because it was so smelly.

When he got home he had another nice hot bath and washed his ears (all three; just to be sure they were all clean). He also washed both of his feet.

His left foot was still a bit stinky but that's OK; that's normal for Trevor, The Rabbit with Three Ears.

Chapter 26

Soapy Slide

One day, Trevor decided he needed to wash the floorboards in the hall of this flat. He filled a basin with hot, soapy water and got down on his knees to start scrubbing the floor.

Just then, his friend Declan arrived. Declan did not know that the floor was wet and slippy. He walked into the hall and immediately skidded along with one leg up in the air. He crashed into the bathroom door at the end of the hall and ended up lying on his back with both his feet above his head.

"Declan!" cried Trevor "are you OK?"

Declan picked himself up and said "That was great! I want to do it again!"

Trevor splashed some more soapy bubbles on the floor and Declan ran and slid along the hall again.

"Wee-Hee", cried Declan "Come on Trevor, you have a go!"

Trevor took a run up and tried to slide but his stinky left foot did not slide as well as his nice right one. He kept falling on his face when he tried to slide. But, don't worry, Trevor soon had a 'good idea'. He got two bars of soap from the bathroom and tied them to his feet. This made them both very slippy and the two rabbit friends had a great time sliding along the hall floor.

The only problem was that they kept banging into the bathroom door.

"Ouch, that's the only bad bit about sliding: when you have to stop" said Declan.

Then Trevor had another 'good idea'. He opened the bathroom door and put some soapy bubbles on the floor. He fetched a tea-tray from the kitchen and put it at a slope against the side of the bath. He then poured some warm water in the bottom of the bath to make a good landing pool.

And they were off!

The two friends were sliding along the hall, right through the bathroom door, up the tray and into the bath with a huge SPLASH!

As the water splashed out of the bath it wet the two bars of soap on Trevor's feet to make them more and more slippy. He zoomed along the hall at great speed and did a somersault into the bath. Declan was using his ten ears as a propeller to make him go faster too.

They were having such great fun that they did not notice all the water sloshing about on the floor. Suddenly, there was a bang at the door and the rabbit from the flat downstairs came barging in.

"What's going on? There's water running down through my ceiling downstairs!"

When he saw what Trevor and Declan were up to, he was not angry anymore and wanted to join in the game.

They all had a great time but eventually decided that they needed to tidy up a bit.

They mopped up most of the splashed water with towels and then Declan used his ears as a fan to blow air to dry up the rest. It was just like the hand-driers in a toilet but without the nasty noise they make.

They were all exhausted and decided to have a cup of tea to relax before going downstairs to help Trevor's neighbour to mop up the water in his flat too.

Chapter 27

Stop Thief

Trevor and Declan were shopping at the Gyle Centre. They went into the big department store beside the carpark and were having fun looking at all the dummy clothes models. Some had no heads, some had no arms and some had no legs.

Trevor challenged one with no legs to a race around the shop. Declan thought this was funny because the dummy had no legs. It couldn't run!

Trevor then tried to shake hands with a dummy which had no arms and Declan has holding his sides, laughing. But, when Trevor went up to one of the models which had no head and offered it a bite of his carrot, Declan was howling with laughter and rolling on the floor of the shop!

Next, Trevor did the trick with the shop mirror which his Grampa had shown him. He stood with the long edge of the mirror right down the middle of this face and body so that the reflection made it look like Declan could see his whole body. When he lifted the leg which Declan could see, the reflection made it look like both of Trevor's legs were off the ground and he was floating in the air.

"Ha, Ha, Ha!" Declan cried "Look everyone, Trevor is floating".

Next, Trevor pulled his three ears to the front of the mirror and said, "Look, I'm Trevor, the rabbit with SIX ears!"

Just then, Trevor spotted an orange tail disappearing behind one of the clothes models. *Who do you think it was? YES, IT WAS THE SLY FOX!*

Trevor saw the fox taking a hat from a model (this one did have a head). He saw the fox putting the hat on his own head. The naughty fox was trying to pretend he had already bought the hat; he was planning to steal it.

"Hey, put that hat back", shouted Trevor and the fox started to run towards the door of the shop.

But, Trevor and Declan were too quick for him. They got to the door first and made a barrier with all of their ears. The fox could not get under or over or round the rabbit barrier so he had to stop running.

The shop policeman arrived and made the fox give back the hat.

As a reward for helping to stop the thief, the policeman said they could each choose something from the shop to take home.

Declan chose a dummy model (one with a head) so that he could stick some of his ears to it. He didn't need all ten of his ears when he was sleeping and they got dirty if he just left them lying on the floor of his bedroom.

Trevor asked for one of the long mirrors so he could practise his 'floating' trick at home.

Chapter 28

Ladders and Snakes

One rainy afternoon, Trevor and Declan were playing Snakes and Ladders in Trevor's flat. The two rabbit friends were busy throwing the dice and moving their counters on the board; sliding up ladders and down snakes. Everything was normal; but not for long!

Suddenly, the big snake whose head was in square 81 and whose tail was in square 23 started to move! It slid right off the board onto the table. Very soon, all the other snakes had slid off the board too.

"What's going on?" said Trevor.

The big snake replied, "We're fed up being the bad guys. Everyone likes the ladders because they help you move up the board towards the winning square. But the snakes make you slide back down again, so nobody likes us. It's not fair!"

"That's a shame," said Trevor, "but wait, I've got a good idea! Why don't you get back onto to board upside-down with your heads at the bottom and your tails at the top? Then we can go up the snakes and down the ladders."

The snakes all had a little chat and agreed they would give it a try. They slithered back onto the board to their usual places but with their heads and tails reversed. The ladders did not need to change since their tops and bottoms are the same as each other.

"Right, we're ready" said the big snake and Trevor and Declan started playing again, going up snakes and down ladders.

Everything was OK for a while but then the little snake between squares 34 and 13 started to slide down to the bottom of the board. Then all the other snakes did the same. There was a big pile of snakes along the bottom row of the board.

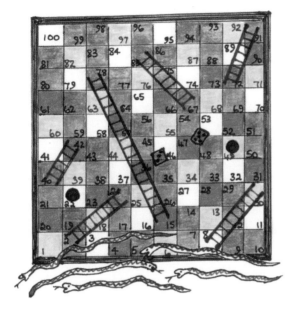

"What's going on, now?" asked Trevor.

"Oh, it's too hard being upside down; we're all getting dizzy", said the big snake.

Then Trevor had another 'good idea'.

"Well, you don't actually need to be upside down for us to go up the snakes. We can just go up from the tail to the head and down the ladders from top to bottom."

"Ok, let's try that," said the big snake. So they all slid back into place and Trevor and Declan continued with their game.

Everyone was happy;

- the snakes were the good guys
- the ladders didn't care
- the rabbits had two different games to play.

From then on, every time they played a game they would decide whether to go up or down the snakes.

If they went down the snakes, they called it 'Snakes and Ladders'.

If they went up the snakes, they called it 'Ladders and Snakes'.

Chapter 29

Tricky Rabbits

One day, Declan had invited his friend, Trevor, round to his house in Leith to play a game of Ladders and Snakes. Declan decided he would play a trick on Trevor. Before Trevor arrived, Declan opened his front door a little bit and put a cushion on top of it, leaning against the wall above.

When Trevor arrived, he pushed the door open and the cushion fell on his head. He got a fright but soon joined Declan in laughing at the trick.

The next time Declan came to visit in Portobello, Trevor played the same trick on him.

This time the cushion landed on Declan's head and bounced off his ten ears. It shot up the hall and hit Trevor right in the face with a SMACK!

"GRRRRR", said Trevor but he was soon laughing again.

A few minutes later, Trevor's phone rang. It was Mrs O'Hare from the flat next door.

"I was just calling to check that you were in because I'd like to come to see you", she said.

"Yes, that's fine, Mrs No Hair … I mean Mrs O'Hare, please come over", said Trevor.

Declan was giggling because they secretly called the neighbour 'Mrs No Hair' as she was very old and was getting a bit bald *(like Trevor's Grampa)*. No-one had ever called her 'Mrs No Hair' when she could hear it! She did not make any comment on his cheeky remark so the rabbits thought she may not have heard it. Her hearing was not as good as it used to be.

"Quick," shouted Trevor to Declan "Mrs No Hair is coming in. Put the cushion up above the door!"

So they set up the trap and when the doorbell rang Trevor shouted "It's open. Come on in!"

Mrs O'Hare opened the door and the cushion fell on her head. She got such a fright that the jar of jam which she had brought for Trevor went flying up in the air. Trevor made a magnificent dive and caught the jar with his three ears. The jar did not smash but the lid must have come loose because he soon noticed that he had strawberry jam running down his face.

"You young scamps!" said Mrs O'Hare, "Perhaps that will teach you not to play tricks on an old rabbit. Now, I'll leave you to tidy up this mess. Goodbye!" and she stormed out of Trevor's flat, slamming the door behind her.

Trevor started to fill the sink with water to wash the jam off his head when Declan went very white and said:

"Look at the label on the jam jar, Trevor".

When Trevor looked he saw that it said:

Strawberry Jam

Made with love for my neighbour Trevor

From 'MRS NO HAIR'

She must have heard them calling her that name after all!

Chapter 30

Ginger George

The Dancing Rabbit Chorus were rehearsing one evening at Trevor's flat when suddenly the living-room door opened a bit and a little orange face appeared in the gap. The smaller rabbits were scared because they thought it was the sly fox coming to play more tricks on them. Then the door opened a bit more and a ginger cat walked in. He stretched his legs out to the front and back showing off that he was the longest cat in Portobello.

"Come in", said Trevor, "do you want to join the chorus?"

"MYEH" said the cat.

"What's your name?" Trevor asked.

"MYEH" said the cat, again.

That's the trouble with cats: no-one really knows what they're thinking or saying.

Mrs O'Hare said that she recognised him; that he often visited the back garden of the flats. No-one knew where he came from and since he had no collar on, no-one knew his real name.

She said that she called him 'Ginger George'.

"Hello again, George", she said as he rolled over onto his back so she could tickle his tummy. He seemed to like that (but then, you never know).

"Do you want to sing?" asked Trevor, politely.

"MYEH" said the cat and he wandered over and picked up Trevor's guitar. Ginger George just stared at all the rabbits as if waiting for them to do something, so they started to sing.

They sang 'the Little Green Frog' song and George strummed the guitar along with them.

The chorus then sang 'Twinkle, Twinkle, Little Star' and again George played along perfectly.

Ginger George was very, very good at playing the guitar and it seemed that he could play any tune the chorus sang.

Trevor was surprised that cats could play guitars but then he noticed that George was using the claws *(or 'clooks' as Trevor's Granny called them)* of one paw to pluck the strings and the flat pads of his other paw to press the strings.

"Why don't you teach us a new song?" Trevor suggested.

Ginger George thought hard for a moment then started playing the guitar and singing along ... *(Well sort of singing)*

The rabbits could recognise the tune as 'Nowhere Man' by the Beatles but instead of singing:

"He's a real Nowhere Man", the cat sang:

"MYEH, MYEH, MYEH, MYEH, MYEH, MYEH"

Some rabbits started to giggle but Trevor joined in singing "MYEH, MYEH, MYEH, MYEH, MYEH, MYEH" too. Soon the whole rabbit chorus became a cats' chorus. It was great fun!

Suddenly, Ginger George put the guitar back on its stand, flicked his tail in the air and walked straight out of the door.

Who knew where he was going?

Who knew if or when he'd be back?

Who knew what his real name was?

You just never know with cats.

30820959R00040

Printed in Poland
by Amazon Fulfillment
Poland Sp. z o.o., Wrocław